Learning to Read, Step by Step!

Ready to Read   Preschool–Kindergarten
• big type and easy words • rhyme and rhythm • picture clues
For children who know the alphabet and are eager to begin reading.

Reading with Help   Preschool–Grade 1
• basic vocabulary • short sentences • simple stories
For children who recognize familiar words and sound out new words with help.

Reading on Your Own   Grades 1–3
• engaging characters • easy-to-follow plots • popular topics
For children who are ready to read on their own.

Reading Paragraphs   Grades 2–3
• challenging vocabulary • short paragraphs • exciting stories
For newly independent readers who read simple sentences with confidence.

Ready for Chapters   Grades 2–4
• chapters • longer paragraphs • full-color art
For children who want to take the plunge into chapter books but still like colorful pictures.

STEP INTO READING® is designed to give every child a successful reading experience. The grade levels are only guides; children will progress through the steps at their own speed, developing confidence in their reading. The F&P Text Level on the back cover serves as another tool to help you choose the right book for your child.

Remember, a lifetime love of reading starts with a single step!

For Olivia,
my wonderful wanderer,
with much love

Text copyright © 2017 by Penguin Random House LLC

Photograph credits: Cover: Grigorita Ko/Shutterstock.com; pp. 1, 9, 10 (bottom), 32: Zuzule/ Shutterstock.com; pp. 3, 31: iStock/Zocha_K; pp. 4–5: iStock/Eric Isselee; p. 6: Lapina/Shutterstock .com; p. 7: iStock/Delpixart; pp. 8, 20: Vera Zinkova/Shutterstock.com; pp. 10 (top), 14 (top): iStock/ mauinow1; p. 11 (top): iStock/Moorefan; p. 11 (bottom): Jeff Gynane/Shutterstock.com; p. 12: Eric Isselee/Shutterstock.com; p. 13: Lenkadan/Shutterstock.com; p. 14 (bottom): iStock/can72; p. 15 (top): Steven Cole/Shutterstock.com; p. 15 (bottom): Christian Mueller/Shutterstock.com; pp. 16, 17: Maria Gaellman/Shutterstock.com; pp. 18, 22, 28, 29: Rita Kochmarjova/Shutterstock.com; p. 19: rokopix/Shutterstock.com; p. 21: iStock/Gannet77; p. 23: iStock/Robert Adrian Hillman; p. 24: iStock/goce; p. 25: Anastasija Popova/Shutterstock.com; p. 26: iStock/AtWaG; p. 27: Boligolov Andrew/Shutterstock.com; p. 30: Phovoir/Shutterstock.com

Visit us on the Web!
StepIntoReading.com
randomhousekids.com

Educators and librarians, for a variety of teaching tools, visit us at RHTeachersLibrarians.com

Library of Congress Cataloging-in-Publication Data
Names: Roberts, Angela, author.
Title: Ponies! / by Angela Roberts.
Description: New York: Penguin Random House LLC, [2017]
Series: Step into reading. Step 2 | Audience: Ages 4–6.
Identifiers: LCCN 2017001667 (print) | LCCN 2017024344 (ebook) |
ISBN 978-1-5247-1440-6 (pb) | ISBN 978-1-5247-1441-3 (glb) | ISBN 978-1-5247-1442-0 (ebk)
Subjects: LCSH: Ponies—Juvenile literature.
Classification: LCC SF315 (ebook) | LCC SF315 .R5 2017 (print) | DDC 636.1/6—dc23

Printed in the United States of America
10 9 8 7 6 5 4 3 2 1

This book has been officially leveled by using the F&P Text Level Gradient™ Leveling System.

STEP INTO READING®

A SCIENCE READER

STEP 2
READING WITH HELP

Ponies!

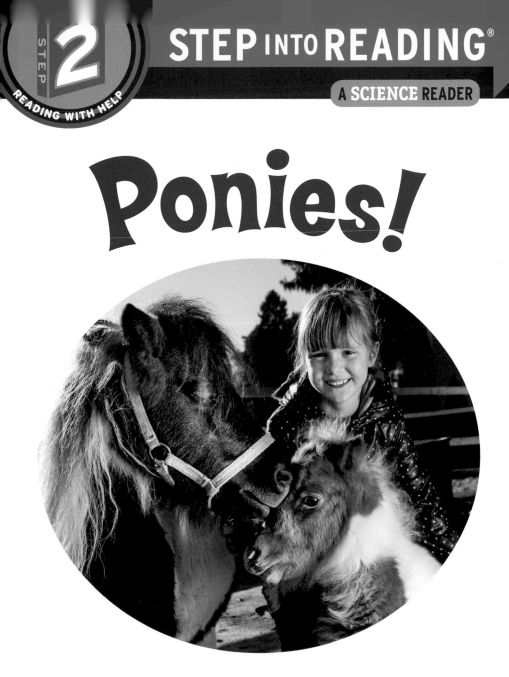

by Angela Roberts

Random House New York

Peachtree

Ponies are cute!
They are smaller
than horses.

mane

Ponies have
soft manes.

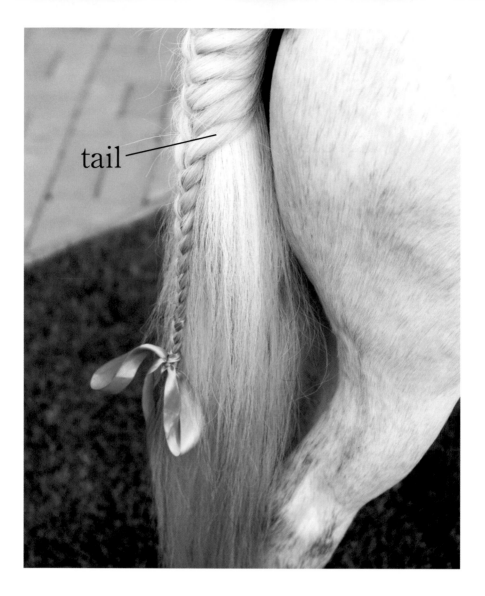

tail

They have thick tails.

This tail is braided.

So fancy!

Ponies also have
thick coats.
Their coats
must be brushed.

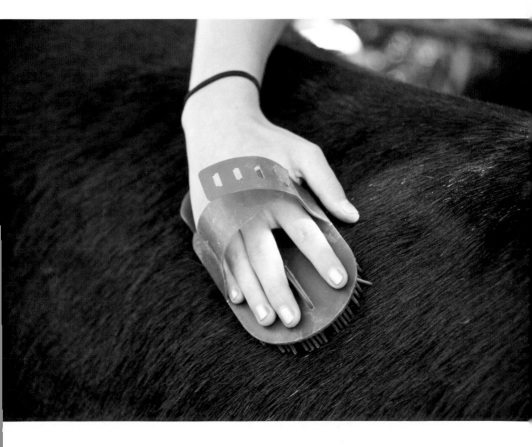

Pretty pony!

There are many breeds
of ponies.

Welsh

Breed means a kind of pony.

Exmoor

Shetland

Each breed of pony looks a bit different.

Dartmoor

New Forest

A young pony
is called a foal.

This foal gets a cuddle
from his mother.
His mother
is called a mare.

Ponies like to eat
grass and hay.

They need to drink
lots of water.
A carrot is a
yummy treat!

Ponies love to play.

Ponies can trot slowly.

They can also gallop fast!

A pony can jump high!

Your pony can win
a prize.

Some ponies do tricks.

Other ponies help people.
These ponies carry
heavy packs.

A saddle helps you
ride a pony.

saddle

shoe / \ hoof

Some ponies wear shoes.
The shoes protect
their hooves.

A pony may lie down
to rest.

A pony can also sleep standing up!

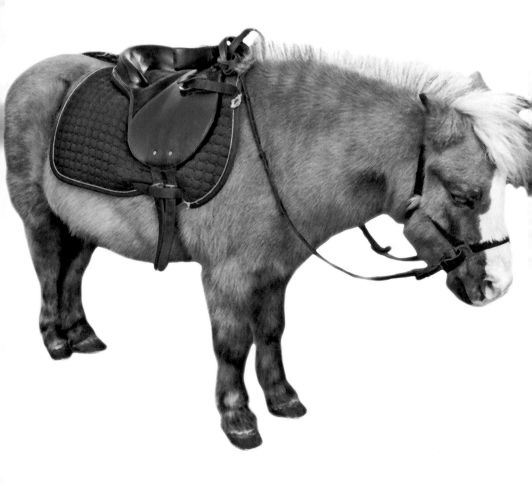

A pony is a good pal.

Hug a pony.

Love a pony!

Ponies are the best!